Securing the Creative Cyberspace

MOHAMED FAWZI ELGENDI

WWW.FAWZOOZ.AI

Copyright © 2024 Mohamed Fawzi Elgendi

No part of this work may be reproduced, distributed, transmitted in any form or by any means, including photocopying, recording, or other electronic or mechanical methods, without the prior written permission of the author, except in the case of brief quotations embodied in critical reviews and certain other noncommercial uses permitted by copyright law with the source duly credited. The names, characters, businesses, places, events, locales, and incidents are either the products of the author's imagination or used in a fictitious manner. Any resemblance to actual persons, living or dead, or actual events is purely coincidental.
www.mohamedfawzi.net

Table of Contents

Preface 5

Chapter 1: Understanding Information Security 10

Chapter 2: ISO 27001 Framework 15

Chapter 3: Risk Management 20

Chapter 4: Implementing Security Controls 25

Chapter 5: Maintaining and Improving Security 30

Chapter 6: Legal and Ethical Considerations 35

Chapter 7: Future of Creative Security 40

Chapter 8: Vulnerability Assessment and Penetration Testing (VAPT) .. 45

Chapter9: Security for Freelance and Remote Creative Work 50

Conclusion 57

Case Study: Implementing ISO 27001 at ISD Software Solutions 62

ABOUT THE AUTHOR 71

2024

PREFACE
WWW.MOHAMEDFAWZI.NET

SECURING THE CREATIVE CYBERSPACE

Preface

Welcome to "Securing the Creative Cyberspace: Leveraging ISO 27001 for Innovation," a pioneering exploration of the intersection between information security and creative processes. As we navigate through an era marked by unprecedented digital advancements, the security of information has become a paramount concern, not only for traditional IT sectors but also within the realms of creativity and innovation.

In creative industries—ranging from digital arts and software development to multimedia and advertising—the sanctity of intellectual properties, customer data, and internal communications is vital. These elements are the lifeblood that fuels innovation and sustains competitive advantage. However, the increasingly complex cyberspace brings with it a host of security challenges that can stifle creativity and erode trust.

This book aims to demystify the principles of ISO 27001, an esteemed global standard for information security management, and present it as an invaluable framework for creative enterprises. By adopting ISO 27001, organizations can not only protect their creative assets but also foster a security culture that supports and enhances the creative process.

The journey through these pages will introduce you to fundamental security concepts tailored to the creative sector, practical guidance on implementing robust security measures, and strategic insights into balancing compliance with creativity. Whether you are a startup founder, a digital innovator, or a leader in a creative agency, this book is designed to equip you with the knowledge and tools to secure your creative environment effectively.

Let us embark on this journey to secure the creative cyberspace, ensuring that our innovative potentials are safeguarded and propelled by the best practices in information security. Together, we will learn how to integrate ISO 27001 into our

creative projects, ensuring that our ventures not only thrive in the present but are also resilient into the future.

This book is not just for CEOs, entrepreneurs, or innovators. It is for anyone who believes in the power of ideas and is looking for ways to adapt to and lead through change. Whether you are a manager in a multinational corporation, a teacher in a bustling classroom, a designer in a startup, or a government official in public service, the insights within these pages are meant to provoke thought, inspire action, and encourage the kind of forward-thinking necessary to thrive in today's complex landscape.

As you turn these pages, I invite you to reflect on the challenges and opportunities in your own environments. Consider this book a companion in your creative endeavors, a source of inspiration to navigate the ever-evolving demands of your professional and personal lives. Let's embrace the constant of change and, together, capture the fleeting, potent ideas that could define the future.

Welcome to a journey of discovery, understanding, and empowerment. Welcome to " Securing the Creative Cyberspace: Leveraging ISO 27001 for Innovation. "

UNDERSTANDING INFORMATION SECURITY

Chapter 1: Understanding Information Security

In the digital age, information security has become a cornerstone of operational integrity across all sectors. For creative industries, where intellectual property serves as the foundation of innovation and competitiveness, securing sensitive data is both a strategic necessity and a challenge. This chapter introduces the core concepts of information security and underscores their importance in nurturing a secure and productive creative environment.

The Pillars of Information Security

1. **Confidentiality**: Ensuring that information is accessible only to those authorized to have access. In creative industries, confidentiality prevents the unauthorized disclosure of new designs, scripts, project details, and client information, safeguarding both the creative process and market competitiveness.

2. **Integrity**: Protecting information from being altered by unauthorized parties and ensuring that it is trustworthy and accurate. For creatives, integrity means that the original ideas, artworks, and communications remain unchanged unless modifications are made by authorized individuals.

3. **Availability**: Ensuring that information and resources are accessible to authorized users when needed. In creative settings, availability supports operational continuity, allowing designers, artists, and developers to access tools and data essential for their work without interruption.

Relevance to Creativity

Securing information not only complies with legal standards but also enhances the creative process:

- **Trust and Collaboration**: Secure environments foster greater collaboration among teams as individuals feel more confident

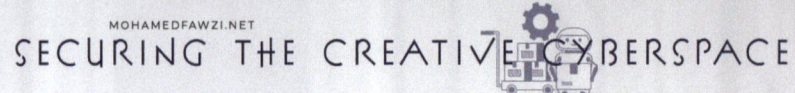

sharing ideas when they know their contributions are protected.

- **Innovation Safety**: Creatives can experiment and innovate without fear of theft or sabotage, knowing their novel ideas are safeguarded by robust security measures.

- **Brand Protection**: Security breaches can damage a company's reputation severely. By protecting sensitive data, creative businesses maintain their brand's integrity and customer trust.

Challenges in Creative Industries

Creative sectors face unique security challenges:

- **High Turnover of Project-Based Work**: Frequent changes in teams with varying access requirements can complicate information control.

- **Collaboration with External Parties**: Working with freelancers, contractors, and partners increases the risk of data leakage if not managed properly.

- **Large Volumes of Data**: Creative projects often generate vast amounts of data, making comprehensive data management and security a complex task.

Understanding the core principles of information security is the first step towards creating a secure framework within which creativity can flourish. As we delve deeper into ISO 27001 in the next chapter, we will explore how these principles can be systematically implemented to not only protect but also enhance the creative processes within your organization.

Chapter 2: ISO 27001 Framework

ISO 27001 is recognized globally as the benchmark for establishing, implementing, maintaining, and continually improving an information security management system (ISMS). For creative industries, adopting this framework can significantly enhance their security posture while fostering a culture of continuous improvement. This chapter provides an in-depth look at ISO 27001, its components, and its particular relevance to creative sectors.

ISO 27001 Explained

ISO 27001 is structured around a systematic approach to managing sensitive company information so that it remains secure. It includes people, processes, and IT systems by applying a risk management process. This standard can help organizations of any kind, in any sector, protect information assets in a systematic and cost-effective way.

Key Components of ISO 27001

1. **Scope of the ISMS:** Define what information you need to protect, considering the creative content and data essential to business operations.

2. **Leadership and Commitment**: The success of an ISMS depends on leadership driving the initiative and supporting the organization through policy development and resource allocation.

3. **Planning**: Identify potential threats to your creative assets and vulnerabilities in your systems that could be exploited. Assess risks systematically and decide on the necessary security measures.

4. **Support and Operation**: Allocate the necessary resources, train your team, and implement the processes needed to achieve your information security objectives.

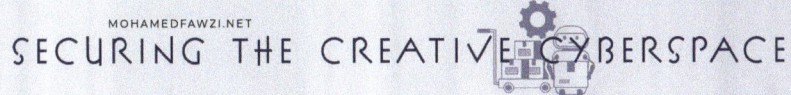

5. **Performance Evaluation**: Regularly review the performance of the ISMS, including internal audits and continuous monitoring, to ensure its effectiveness and adapt to new security challenges.

6. **Improvement**: Based on regular evaluations, make necessary adjustments to enhance the ISMS and address emerging threats.

Benefits of Adopting ISO 27001 in Creative Industries

- **Protection of Intellectual Property:** ISO 27001 helps secure intellectual assets, whether they're designs, scripts, films, or digital files, from theft and sabotage.

- **Enhanced Client Trust:** By demonstrating compliance with an internationally recognized standard, creative firms can build stronger trust with clients who value the security of their data.

- **Regulatory Compliance**: Many regions require compliance with specific data protection standards. ISO 27001 can help meet these regulatory requirements, reducing the risk of legal penalties.

- **Competitive Advantage**: In a market where clients are more aware of data security, ISO 27001 certification can distinguish a company from competitors.

Adopting ISO 27001 provides a structured framework for managing information security in a way that supports the dynamic and innovative nature of creative industries. As organizations continue to evolve and face new security challenges, the principles of ISO 27001 remain relevant, offering a flexible and robust approach to securing creative assets and sensitive information.

Chapter 3: Risk Management

the creative industries, where the currency is innovation and the assets are digital and intellectual, managing risks to these assets is crucial. This chapter delves into the process of identifying, analyzing, and mitigating risks in accordance with ISO 27001, tailored specifically for creative professionals and organizations.

Understanding Risk in Creative Contexts

Risk management in the context of ISO 27001 involves a systematic approach to managing sensitive company information so that it remains secure. It requires an understanding of what your information risks are, where they come from, and how they could impact your business.

Identifying Risks

1. **Asset Identification**: List all assets that are crucial to your creative processes, such as digital files, client databases, and proprietary software.

2. **Threat Assessment**: Identify potential threats to these assets, including cyber-attacks, physical theft, or accidental loss.

3. **Vulnerability Evaluation**: Determine vulnerabilities in your system that might be exploited by threats, such as weak passwords or outdated software.

Analyzing Risks

- **Likelihood and Impact**: Assess the likelihood of each risk occurring and its potential impact on the business. This can help prioritize the risks that need the most attention.

- **Risk Scenarios**: Develop scenarios to understand how specific risks could affect your operations. This is particularly useful in creative settings where new types of projects or technologies might introduce unique risks.

Mitigating Risks

- **Applying Controls**: Implement appropriate controls from ISO 27001 to mitigate identified risks. These might include encryption, access control systems, and regular security audits.

- **Risk Treatment Plan**: Create a risk treatment plan that outlines how you intend to handle each risk – whether you'll mitigate, transfer, avoid, or accept it.

- **Regular Reviews**: Risk management is a dynamic process, especially in creative fields where the technological landscape can change rapidly. Regular reviews ensure that new risks are identified and managed appropriately.

Effective risk management is not just about protecting against losses; it's also about ensuring the sustainability and growth of the creative enterprise. By applying the risk management principles of ISO 27001, creative businesses can not only safeguard their assets but also enhance their decision-making processes and adapt more readily to changes in the marketplace.

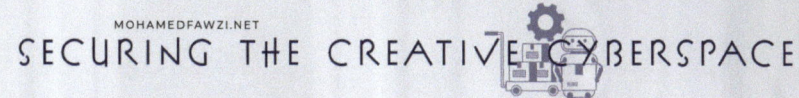

Chapter 4: Implementing Security Controls

After identifying and assessing the risks specific to the creative industries, the next step under ISO 27001 is to implement tailored security controls that effectively mitigate these risks. This chapter outlines the practical aspects of applying these controls, ensuring both compliance with the standard and enhancement of creative workflows.

ISO 27001 Security Control Clusters

ISO 27001 categorizes its recommended controls into several clusters, each addressing different aspects of information security management. These clusters include:

1. **Organization of Information Security**: Establishing governance structures and roles to ensure clear accountability for information security.

2. **Human Resource Security**: Ensuring that employees understand their security responsibilities, which is particularly crucial in industries where staff turnover can be high and project-based.

3. **Asset Management**: Identifying and classifying information assets, which in creative contexts, can range from digital content to client data and proprietary tools.

4. **Access Control**: Restricting access to information and systems to authorized individuals only. In creative agencies, where collaboration with external parties is common, robust access control is vital.

5. **Cryptography**: Using encryption to protect the confidentiality and integrity of sensitive data, especially when it is transmitted over insecure networks or stored on portable devices.

6. **Physical and Environmental Security**: Protecting physical assets from unauthorized access, damage, and interference.

This includes securing physical locations where creative work is performed.

7. **Operations Security**: Implementing proper procedures to ensure correct and secure operations of information processing facilities.

8. **Communications Security**: Securing information in networks and its supporting information processing facilities, crucial for teams that collaborate remotely.

9. **System Acquisition, Development, and Maintenance**: Ensuring that security is an integral part of information systems and that information security is part of the system lifecycle.

10. **Supplier Relationships**: Managing supplier relationships to ensure that suppliers and third-party service providers protect the assets they are accessing or managing.

11. **Information Security Incident Management:** Ensuring a consistent and effective approach to the management of information security incidents, including communication on security events and weaknesses.

12. **Information Security Aspects of Business Continuity Management**: Embedding information security into the organization's business continuity management systems.

13. **Compliance**: Ensuring that the organization complies with all relevant laws, regulations, and contractual obligations.

The successful implementation of ISO 27001 security controls within creative industries not only protects valuable information assets but also supports and enhances the creative process. By integrating these security practices into daily operations, creative organizations can ensure that their innovations are secure and their operations compliant, giving them a competitive edge in the market.

MAINTAINING AND IMPROVING SECURITY

Chapter 5: Maintaining and Improving Security

With the implementation of security controls under ISO 27001, the ongoing task is to maintain and continually improve the information security management system (ISMS). This chapter discusses strategies for sustaining effective security practices and adapting to evolving risks in the creative industries.

Continuous Improvement Through ISO 27001

ISO 27001 emphasizes a continuous improvement model known as Plan-Do-Check-Act (PDCA). This model facilitates ongoing evaluation and refinement of the ISMS, ensuring it remains effective in the face of new challenges and changes in the organization.

1. **Plan:** Establish objectives and processes necessary to deliver results in accordance with the organization's information security policy.

2. **Do:** Implement and operate the processes as planned.

3. **Check**: Monitor and review the processes against the security policy, objectives, and practical experience, and report the results.

4. **Act**: Take actions to continually improve the performance of the ISMS.

Strategies for Maintaining Security

- **Regular Audits and Reviews**: Conduct regular internal and external audits to ensure compliance with ISO 27001 and to identify areas for improvement.

- **Security Training and Awareness**: Continuously educate and train employees about security policies, emerging threats, and safe practices, particularly important in creative fields where technology and collaborative tools evolve rapidly.

- **Technology Updates and Management**: Keep security technologies and systems updated to protect against new vulnerabilities and to incorporate advanced security features.

Adapting to New Threats

Creative industries often employ cutting-edge technologies and collaborative platforms that can introduce unique security challenges. Adapting the ISMS to these evolving risks is crucial.

- **Threat Intelligence**: Stay informed about new and emerging threats specifically targeting creative content and intellectual property.

- **Flexible Security Policies**: Develop security policies that can adapt to the changing nature of creative work and technology use.

Maintaining and improving the security of information within the creative industries is an ongoing journey that requires vigilance, adaptation, and a commitment to continuous improvement. By employing the PDCA cycle and staying agile in the face of new security challenges, creative organizations can protect their assets and foster a culture of security that supports their innovative endeavors.

LEGAL AND ETHICAL CONSIDERATIONS

Chapter 6: Legal and Ethical Considerations

In the realm of creative industries, where innovation is at the forefront, legal and ethical considerations form a critical backbone of information security practices. This chapter explores the intricate relationship between compliance with legal standards, ethical data handling, and the cultivation of trust in creative enterprises.

Navigating Legal Compliance

Adhering to legal standards is not only a matter of regulatory compliance but also a strategic necessity in protecting the organization and its clients. ISO 27001 supports compliance by providing a structured framework to manage sensitive information, helping to meet various legal obligations.

1. **Data Protection Regulations**: The General Data Protection Regulation (GDPR) in Europe and similar laws worldwide significantly impact creative industries, requiring explicit consent for personal data use and ensuring strict compliance in how this data is managed and utilized for creating personalized content.

2. **Intellectual Property Laws**: Intellectual property laws are crucial for safeguarding creative works from theft or misuse. ISO 27001 helps protect these assets by establishing security controls and procedures that prevent unauthorized access and ensure the integrity of creative content.

3. **Contractual Obligations**: ISO 27001 plays a crucial role in helping organizations meet contractual obligations related to information security, enhancing compliance and fostering trust with clients and partners by demonstrating a commitment to protecting sensitive data.

Ethical Challenges in Creative Industries

Ethical considerations are vital in industries that deal with creative content. Key issues include:

- **Confidentiality and Privacy**: It's crucial to maintain confidentiality, especially for projects involving sensitive data, to protect individual privacy and project integrity.

- **Transparency**: Achieving a balance between protecting information and being transparent about data handling practices is essential for building stakeholder trust.

- **Respecting Copyrights and Creative Rights**: Properly handling creative content, ensuring respect for original creators' rights through appropriate licensing and crediting, is necessary to avoid legal and ethical issues.

These challenges underscore the need for robust ethical policies to ensure the integrity and fairness of creative industries.

Implementing Ethical Practices

Integrating ethical considerations into daily information security practices is crucial for fostering a culture of ethical awareness within organizations.

- **Ethical Decision-Making Frameworks:** Implement decision-making frameworks to help staff handle complex information security and ethical dilemmas, ensuring decisions align with organizational values and ethics.

- **Whistleblower Protections**: Promote an open environment with robust whistleblower protections to allow employees to report unethical or illegal practices without fear of retaliation, ensuring a transparent and accountable workplace.

Incorporating ethical practices into information security management is vital for compliance and preserving the integrity and reputation of organizations, especially in creative industries where trust and credibility are essential.

FUTURE OF
CREATIVE SECURITY.

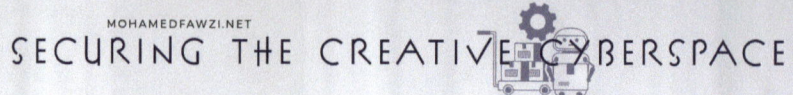

Chapter 7: Future of Creative Security

As the digital landscape continues to evolve at a rapid pace, so too does the field of information security within the creative industries. This chapter explores the emerging trends and technologies that are shaping the future of creative security, offering insights into how organizations can remain resilient and innovative in the face of these changes.

Emerging Technologies and Their Impact

The integration of cutting-edge technologies is transforming how creative content is produced, shared, and protected. Here are some key technologies to consider:

1. Artificial Intelligence (AI): AI can automate complex security tasks such as real-time threat detection and response. It also poses new challenges, such as ensuring the security of AI-

generated content and protecting AI systems from manipulation.

2. Blockchain: This technology offers new ways to manage copyright and intellectual property rights, providing a transparent and immutable ledger for creative assets.

3. Internet of Things (IoT): As creative tools become more connected, IoT security becomes crucial in protecting these devices from becoming entry points for security breaches.

Adapting Security Strategies for Tomorrow

As technology evolves, so must our security strategies to protect new innovations. Key approaches include:

- **Proactive Security Measures**: it is Important to integrate security early in the design phase of new technologies to preempt vulnerabilities and ensure foundational security.

- **Continuous Learning and Adaptation**: Organizations must stay informed about the latest security technologies and methodologies, continuously updating their security practices and training to address evolving threats effectively.

These strategies highlight the necessity of foresight and continuous improvement in maintaining effective security measures as technology advances.

Building a Culture of Security Innovation

To effectively respond to the dynamic nature of security threats, creative industries need to foster a culture where security innovation is as valued as creative innovation.

- **Encouraging Experimentation**: Promoting a culture where experimenting with new security solutions is encouraged, and where failures are seen as learning opportunities.

- **Collaboration Across Disciplines:** Facilitating collaboration between security professionals and creative teams to ensure that security solutions enhance, rather than hinder, the creative process.

The future of creative security is not just about defending against threats but also about enabling new forms of creative expression through innovative security practices. By embracing the changes brought about by emerging technologies and fostering a culture of proactive security innovation, creative industries can not only protect their assets but also lead the way in the development of new, secure creative technologies.

VULNERABILITY ASSESSMENT AND PENETRATION TESTING

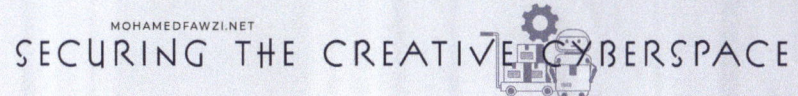

Chapter 8: Vulnerability Assessment and Penetration Testing (VAPT)

In an era where digital threats are increasingly sophisticated, Vulnerability Assessment and Penetration Testing (VAPT) provide crucial defenses for any organization's security posture. This chapter focuses on how creative industries can employ VAPT to identify, assess, and remediate security vulnerabilities in their systems and applications, ensuring that their innovative outputs are safeguarded against potential attacks.

VAPT consists of two main components:

1. **Vulnerability Assessment**: This process involves the systematic review of security weaknesses in an information system. It evaluates if the system is susceptible to any known vulnerabilities, assigns severity levels to those vulnerabilities, and recommends remediation or mitigation techniques.

2. **Penetration Testing**: Unlike vulnerability assessments, penetration testing (or ethical hacking) is an active process. It simulates an attack from a malicious hacker. The goal is to understand how well the system can defend itself, and what potential data could be extracted by successful hackers.

Relevance to Creative Industries

Creative sectors often deal with a vast amount of intellectual property that, if compromised, could lead to significant financial and reputational damage. Employing VAPT allows these industries to:

- **Identify** vulnerabilities in their creative tools and platforms before they can be exploited.

- **Ensure** the integrity and availability of digital assets such as multimedia content, designs, scripts, and other proprietary information.

- **Comply** with industry regulations and standards that mandate regular security assessments.

Implementing VAPT in Creative Settings

- **Planning and Scoping:** Determine what systems, networks, and data need to be tested based on their sensitivity and exposure risk.

- **Choosing the Right Tools and Techniques**: Select tools and methodologies appropriate for the creative environment, considering the technologies used and the nature of the work.

- **Execution and Reporting**: Conduct the tests and document the findings. Reports should clearly outline discovered vulnerabilities, the risks associated with these vulnerabilities, and the recommended actions to address them.

Challenges and Best Practices

- **Keeping Pace with New Vulnerabilities**: As new technologies are adopted, new vulnerabilities emerge. Continuous learning and adaptation of VAPT strategies are necessary.

- **Integrating Security into the Creative Process**: Security should be a seamless aspect of the creative process, not a hindrance. Balancing security concerns with usability is key.

- **Ethical Considerations**: Ensure that all penetration testing is conducted ethically and legally, with proper authorization and within defined boundaries.

Vulnerability Assessment and Penetration Testing are not just technical necessities but strategic imperatives in the protection of creative content and systems. By understanding and implementing VAPT, creative industries can proactively manage their security risks, ensuring that their creative outputs are not only innovative but also secure from potential threats.

SECURITY FOR FREELANCE AND REMOTE CREATIVE WORK

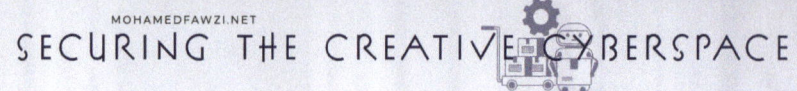

Chapter9: Security for Freelance and Remote Creative Work

The rise of freelance and remote work has transformed the creative industries, allowing for unprecedented flexibility and access to global talent. However, this shift also introduces significant security challenges as creatives often work outside the controlled environment of a traditional office. This chapter explores the unique security risks associated with remote and freelance creative work and provides strategies to mitigate these risks, with a particular focus on leveraging cloud security solutions.

Understanding the Risks

Remote and freelance creatives typically rely on personal devices and home networks, which may not be as secure as those in an office setting. The primary risks include:

1. **Insecure Networks**: Home Wi-Fi systems and public networks may lack robust security, exposing data to interception.

2. **Device Theft and Loss:** Personal devices used for work are more susceptible to theft or can be easily lost, leading to potential data breaches.

3. **Lack of Controlled Access:** Without corporate IT oversight, it's challenging to ensure that only authorized users access sensitive data.

4. **Phishing and Social Engineering Attacks:** Remote workers are often targeted by scams designed to steal credentials or install malware.

Implementing Effective Security Measures

Developing a Comprehensive Security Policy:Freelancers and remote workers should adhere to a clear security policy that outlines:

- Required security measures for devices and networks.

- Guidelines for password management and multi-factor authentication.

- Procedures for securely sharing and storing information.

- Actions to take in case of a security breach.

Securing Networks

- **Use of VPNs**: A virtual private network (VPN) should be mandatory for accessing any work-related resources to encrypt internet traffic and shield data from unauthorized interception.

- **Securing Home Wi-Fi**: Instructions on changing default router settings, using strong Wi-Fi passwords, and regularly updating router firmware to protect against vulnerabilities.

Enhancing Device Security

- **Endpoint Protection:** Installation of reputable antivirus and anti-malware software, with regular updates to defend against new threats.

- **Physical Security Measures**: Use of cable locks, secure storage when not in use, and never leaving devices unattended in public places.

- **Encryption**: Full disk encryption should be enabled on all devices to protect the data in case of theft or loss.

Leveraging Cloud Security for Data Protection

Cloud solutions offer robust tools for securing data and facilitating collaboration:

- **Data Encryption:** Use cloud services that provide end-to-end encryption both in transit and at rest.

- **Access Controls**: Implement strict access controls with role-based permissions to ensure that only authorized individuals can view or modify sensitive data.

- **Regular Backups**: Utilize cloud backup solutions to automatically back up data and protect against data loss due to hardware failure or accidental deletion.

- **Secure Collaboration Tools:** Opt for collaboration platforms that offer enhanced security features, ensuring that file sharing and communications are protected.

Awareness and Training

- **Regular Security Training**: Conduct regular sessions on security best practices, emerging threats, and safe internet habits.

- **Phishing Awareness:** Educate about the risks of phishing attacks and how to recognize suspicious emails or messages.

Adapting to New Technologies

As cloud technologies evolve, it's crucial for freelancers and remote workers to stay informed about new security tools and practices. They should be encouraged to adopt new technologies that enhance security, such as biometric authentication and advanced threat detection systems.

For freelancers and remote workers in the creative industries, understanding and mitigating security risks is crucial for protecting both their work and their clients' data. By implementing robust security policies, securing networks and devices, leveraging cloud security, and maintaining an ongoing commitment to security education, creatives can significantly reduce their vulnerability to cyber threats. This proactive approach to security ensures that the flexibility of remote and freelance work does not come at the cost of data integrity and privacy.

CONCLUSION 2024
WWW.MOHAMEDFAWZI.NET

SECURING THE CREATIVE CYBERSPACE

Conclusion

As we conclude our exploration of "Securing the Creative Cyberspace: Leveraging ISO 27001 for Innovation," it's evident that the intersection of information security and creativity is not only crucial but also dynamic. The synthesis of these disciplines offers creative industries a robust framework to protect their most valuable assets while fostering an environment where innovation can thrive.

Key Takeaways

- **Comprehensive Understanding**: The deep dive into ISO 27001 provided a structured approach to managing and safeguarding information, crucial for maintaining the integrity and confidentiality of creative assets.

- **Risk Management:** Identifying, assessing, and mitigating risks is foundational to sustaining creativity. The application of ISO 27001's risk management principles ensures that creative enterprises can adapt and respond to changes in the security landscape effectively.

- **Legal and Ethical Foundations**: The discussion on legal and ethical considerations highlighted the importance of compliance and ethical handling of information, which not only protects the organization legally but also builds trust with clients and partners.

- **Future-Proofing Security Practices**: Emerging technologies such as AI, blockchain, and IoT are shaping the future of creative security. Staying ahead requires a proactive approach to security, integrating new technologies responsibly and innovatively.

Moving Forward

The journey through securing creative spaces does not end here. As technologies evolve and creative processes become more intricate, the need for a dynamic and responsive

information security management system becomes even more critical. The principles and strategies outlined in this book are not meant to be static but adapted as new challenges and opportunities arise.

Let this book serve as both a guide and an inspiration:

- **For Security Professionals**: To understand and appreciate the unique challenges and opportunities within creative industries, applying ISO 27001 with a perspective that enhances rather than restricts creativity.

- **For Creatives**: To embrace information security as a vital part of the creative process, ensuring that their innovations are protected and their operations are compliant.

- **For Business Leaders**: To advocate for and invest in robust security practices that secure not just data, but also foster an environment where creativity and innovation are at the forefront.

Next Steps

Continue learning, adapting, and innovating. The realm of creativity paired with the discipline of information security offers endless possibilities. It is up to us to navigate these waters wisely and with foresight, ensuring that the digital renaissance in creative industries is both vibrant and secure.

2024

CASE STUDY
WWW.MOHAMEDFAWZI.NET

SECURING THE CREATIVE CYBERSPACE

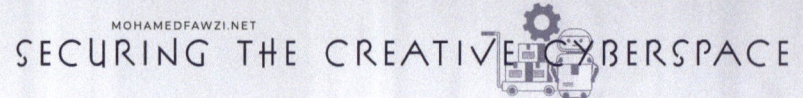

Case Study: Implementing ISO 27001 at ISD Software Solutions

Company Overview

ISD Software Solutions specializes in developing software for remote alarms, monitoring, and situational awareness. Their applications are essential for security and emergency response operations, demanding the highest standards of reliability and security.

Challenges Faced

Before implementing ISO 27001, ISD faced several critical challenges:

- **Vulnerability to Cyber Attacks**: The high stakes associated with their software demanded exceptional protection measures against sophisticated cyber threats.

- **Inconsistent Security Practices**: Varied security protocols across different teams and projects led to potential vulnerabilities.

- **Compliance Pressures**: Adhering to strict regulatory standards was crucial, given the sensitive nature of their operational areas.

ISO 27001 Implementation

ISD recognized the need for a robust Information Security Management System (ISMS) and chose ISO 27001 to standardize and enhance its security practices.

Steps Taken

1. Scope Definition: The ISMS scope included all processes involved in designing, developing, deploying, and supporting software for remote monitoring and situational awareness.

2. Risk Assessment: ISD conducted comprehensive assessments to identify risks specifically associated with software development and deployment.

3. Implementation of Security Controls:

- **Enhanced Access Control**: Rigorous access controls were established to ensure that only authorized personnel could access and modify software code and configurations.

- **Encryption and Data Security**: Advanced encryption was implemented for data transmission and storage, crucial for protecting communication between remote devices and monitoring centers.

- **Secure Development Lifecycle**: Integrated secure software development practices into every phase of the software lifecycle, from initial design to deployment and maintenance. This included regular code reviews, static and dynamic code

analysis, and integration of security testing as a core component of the software development process.

4. Employee Training and Awareness: ISD intensified its training programs, focusing on secure coding practices, common vulnerabilities and exposures in software development, and ways to mitigate these risks.

Results

Post-implementation of ISO 27001, ISD Software Solutions experienced significant improvements:

- **Robust Security Framework**: The incorporation of secure software development practices greatly reduced vulnerabilities at the coding and design levels.

- **Enhanced Operational Reliability**: With stricter security controls and ongoing risk assessments, ISD ensured higher reliability and security of its software, critical for its clients' operations.

- Customer Confidence and Market Growth: Enhanced security measures and compliance with ISO 27001 attracted new customers, particularly in sectors where security is a critical selling point.

Ongoing Improvements

- Continuous Monitoring and Improvement: ISD remains committed to the continuous monitoring and updating of its ISMS to address emerging security threats and changes in technology.

- Adaptation to New Technologies: The company regularly evaluates new security technologies and methodologies to enhance its products and security practices further.

Lesson learned

As the Chief Information Security Officer (CISO), my involvement in the strategic deployment of ISO 27001 at ISD was pivotal in transforming our approach to software security and embedding a robust security culture across the company. This initiative not only enhanced our defenses against potential threats but also established secure software development practices as a fundamental aspect of our Information Security Management System (ISMS).

As a result, ISD has maintained the integrity and security of our software products, underscoring our dedication to delivering secure, high-quality software solutions.

This transformation through ISO 27001 adoption exemplifies its potential to revolutionize an organization's security posture and business success, especially in sectors where software reliability and security are critical.

The positive shifts in our operational strategies have not only strengthened ISD's market presence but have also highlighted the dynamic nature of information security.

Our ongoing efforts to refine our ISMS reflect the necessity of agility in adapting to emerging threats and evolving technologies. Such continuous improvement ensures our security measures keep pace with technological advancements and shifts in the threat landscape.

Furthermore, this case study underscores the advantages of implementing ISO 27001 that extend beyond compliance. It demonstrates how organizations can utilize this standard to cultivate a resilient and proactive security environment, thereby supporting key business goals like customer retention, market expansion, and competitive differentiation.

By prioritizing security within our business strategy, ISD has safeguarded its assets and assured our clients that their critical operations rely on secure and dependable software systems.

This strategic focus has yielded significant business benefits, including enhanced customer trust, increased sales, and a stronger industry reputation.

Overall, ISD's experience serves as a compelling model for other companies in high-stakes fields, showing that a strategic focus on information security management can significantly influence both security and business outcomes.

SECURING THE CREATIVE CYBERSPACE

Mohamed Fawzi Elgendi

me@mohamedfawzi.net
Dubai, UAE

AI Enthusiast & Mental wellness Author

Pioneering Digital Innovation, AI Advancement, and Cybersecurity Excellence.

Chief Information Security Officer (CISO)

Chief Digital and AI Officer (CDAO)

Post Graduate Program in Artificial Intelligence For Leaders

Bachelor's degree in Computer and Systems Engineering

400+ Enterprise project

70+ Training & Workshop

17+ Authored books

16+ Years Experience

- CBT COACH
- EQ
- DBT
- SCRUM
- ISO27001
- DATA SCIENCE
- BUSINESS OF AI
- DIGITAL PRODUCT DEVELOPMENT
- EXECUTIVE LEADERSHIP
- ENTREPRENEURSHIP

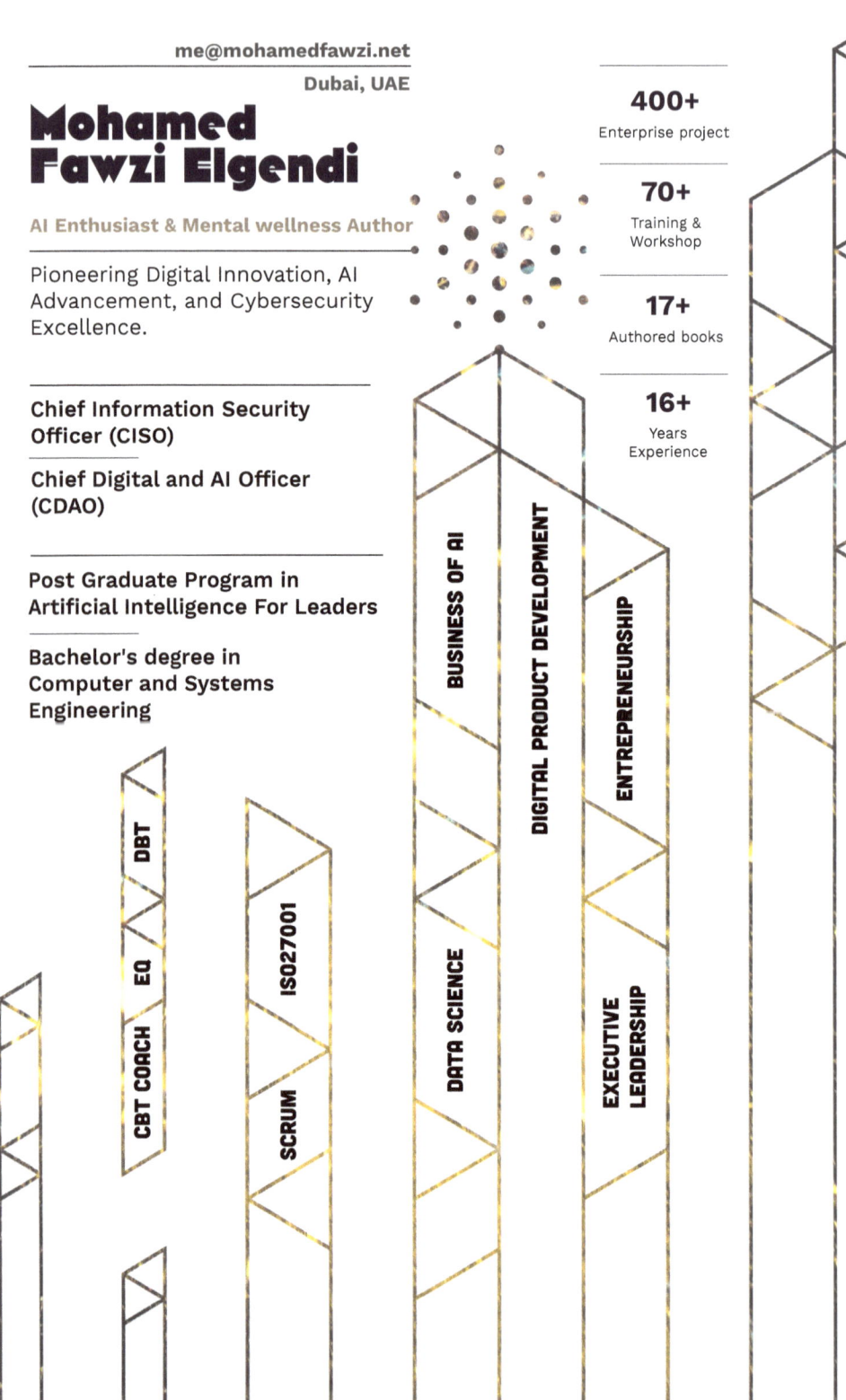

www.ingramcontent.com/pod-product-compliance
Lightning Source LLC
Chambersburg PA
CBHW040229220526
45473CB00001B/177